JOE LOUIS
A CHAMP
FOR ALL AMERICA

ROBERT LIPSYTE

HarperCollins*Publishers*

Acknowledgments

Every effort has been made to locate the copyright holders of all copyrighted materials and secure the necessary permissions to reproduce them. In the event of any questions arising as to their use, the publisher will be glad to make changes in future printings and editions.

In addition, the publisher acknowledges the following institutions for the illustrations provided to us: pages 7, 17, 22, 23, 30, 40, 48, 62, 73, 77, 79, 82–83, and 85: UPI/Bettmann; pages 18, 45, 58, and 71: UPI/Bettmann Newsphotos; and page 52: The Bettmann Archive.

★

Joe Louis
A Champ for All America

Library of Congress Cataloging-in-Publication Data
Lipsyte, Robert.
Joe Louis : a champ for all America / Robert Lipsyte.
  p.   cm. — (Superstar lineup)
Includes bibliographical references and index.
ISBN 0-06-023410-5 (lib. bdg.)
  1. Louis, Joe, 1914–1981—Juvenile literature. 2. Boxers (Sports)—United States—Biography—Juvenile literature. I. Title. II. Series.
GV1132.L6L56 1994   93-48767
796.8'3'092—dc20   CIP
[B]   AC

Typography by Tom Starace
1   2   3   4   5   6   7   8   9   10
❖
First Edition

★

For Sam Lipsyte, my coauthor

★

Tom Molyneux, a slave from Virginia, punched his way to freedom and on to England, where he almost beat the British heavyweight champ, Tom Cribb.

Prologue

The first black athletes in the United States were slaves. They raced thoroughbred horses and fought brutal bare-knuckle boxing matches to entertain plantation masters who bet on them. After the Emancipation Proclamation, they brought their sporting heritage down freedom road.

In the first Kentucky Derby, in 1875, fourteen of the fifteen jockeys were black. The outstanding jockey of the time was Isaac Murphy, a black who won the Derby three times. But by the turn of the century, when horse racing became a major sport and there was big money to be made at it, black jockeys and trainers had been squeezed out. They have yet to return to the racetrack in any great number except as laborers.

Black prizefighters have been discriminated against, too, but their story is a different one.

A Virginia slave, Tom Molyneux, won his freedom in a fight and then traveled to New

York, where he boxed other black free men. Eventually he went to England, where boxing was far more popular. After almost beating Tom Cribb, the white British heavyweight champion, in 1810, he opened his own boxing gym, which became a great success. Not only did Molyneux train young black professionals, some of whom fought in the United States, but he also taught rich fashionable white Londoners who wanted to look and act tough.

By the end of the nineteenth century, boxing was an established sport in the United States. There were famous black fighters, such as Samuel Grant ("The Indiana Darkey") and Peter Jackson ("The Black Prince") and George Godfrey ("Old Chocolate"). But they were simply not given the chance to box the famous whites, such as James J. Corbett or Bob Fitzsimmons or John L. Sullivan.

In fact, "The Great John L.," recognized as the first heavyweight champion of the world, a man famous for bursting into barrooms with the boast "I can lick any man in the house," declared, "I will not fight a Negro. I never have and never shall."

The white establishment did not consider him a coward. One of the leading journalists of the day, Charles A. Dana, in 1895 wrote in the New York *Sun:* "We are in the midst of a growing menace. The black man is rapidly forging to the front rank in athletics, especially in fisticuffs. We are in the midst of a black rise against white supremacy. Just at present, we are safe from the humiliation of having a black man world's champion, but we had a pretty narrow escape."

This was, of course, only thirty years after the Civil War. Laws that discriminated against blacks—the so-called Jim Crow laws—were dismantling black progress. There was segregation in American churches, schools, hotels, trains and toilets. To create a rationale for this vicious discrimination, there were pseudoscientific studies claiming that blacks were mentally and physiologically inferior, that they were subhuman, savage or childlike.

This propaganda campaign would be damaged if a black man beat a white in the ring, especially since John L. Sullivan had promoted himself and his championship as a symbol of virility and honor, as a protector of women and children and as a role model for all those young men who were leaving the farms and coming to the growing big cities of America.

On the day after Christmas, 1908, the menace that journalist Dana was worried about arrived. In Sydney, Australia, Tommy Burns, an Englishman, lost his heavyweight title to a black American named Jack Johnson.

The novelist Jack London, covering the fight from ringside, sent out an urgent call for a white hero, the hope of the race, to "remove the golden smile from Johnson's face."

Jack Johnson kept smiling for another seven years, and America got to know more about a single black man than it had ever known before. Much of white America was outraged by what it saw—a smart, cocky, seemingly fearless black man who spoke his mind, showed no deference to whites and, most threatening of all, openly lived with white women and even married three of them.

But most of black America recognized Jack Johnson as a bold man who didn't react passively. He stood up to discrimination, to segregation, to unfairness in ways that most people could not. He was, in his way, a revolutionary.

Jack Johnson was eventually beaten down in and out of the ring, and white fighters regained control of the heavyweight championship. But he remained a warning and an inspiration for the generations of great black athletes to come.

His story probably affected no athlete more than Joseph Louis Barrow, an Alabama farm boy who grew up to be heavyweight champion of the world for eleven years, eight months—longer than anyone else in history—and became a hero throughout the world for people of every color.

1

The boy was seventeen, six feet tall, lithe and strong. He clutched a battered case under his jacket. Inside was a rented violin.

As he bobbed through the crowds on the avenue, he felt alert and excited. As he wrote later in his autobiography, he sensed that this day could be the turning point in his life. At the corner vegetable stand where he sometimes worked, he saw his old friend Freddie Guinyard, all skin and bones and silver tongue, hustling himself another day's pay. There was noise and light on this cold January afternoon in Detroit, but there was a hard, dead look in people's eyes, too.

It was 1931 and the Great Depression had begun. Millions were out of work, standing in

Joe Louis's family joined the great migration of black southern farmers who went north for factory jobs in the 1920's. By the 1930's, however, the Great Depression threw millions out of work. These two scenes of free food handouts were photographed in New York City.

soup lines, doing whatever they could to feed their families.

He turned onto a side street and stood on the sidewalk in front of a large frame house. He stomped his feet to keep warm. The sweet tinkle of a piano floated through the frost-glazed windows. He heard a jingling in his pants pocket, too, the fifty cents Momma had given him for his music lessons.

He'd bought the pants on his own with the money he saved hauling ice up tenement stairs with Freddie last summer, and Momma would cry if she saw her little Joseph was not wearing his schoolboy knickers anymore. He rolled them up to his knees every time he came home.

And she would cry again if she knew what he was going do.

Joe Barrow strode away from the music teacher's house toward a handsome, wiry kid waiting for him on the corner. Thurston McKinney had been the most popular boy in school, and the most respected. A few years older than Joe, he was the Detroit Golden Gloves welterweight boxing champion. Joe felt proud walking back down the avenue next to this hero.

Thurston had told him how easy it could be. You just go to the boxing gym, train hard, and they set you up with amateur fights. Win or lose, you get a merchandise check, up to twenty-five dollars, which you could cash in for food. What could Momma say then? Even with his stepfather, Pat Brooks, Sr., and Joe's brothers working in the Ford plant, money was scarce. The fifty cents Momma gave him for the violin lessons were just a bet on the future. She said so herself.

"If you practice hard, Joe, maybe you could make something for yourself."

Joe thought of that violin in the case under his jacket. It felt so funny in his big hands, and when he drew the bow across the strings, it made that screechy sound, like when his sisters bickered. At the end of every lesson he was sure his music teacher sighed as he took Joe's money.

Now this is a better bet for the future, Momma, Joe thought. He looked over at Thurston, just a little older but with an easy power to his walk, a good-natured confidence. He'd never start a fight, but you bet he could finish one with anybody.

Thurston had heard Joe could finish some, too. Like that time the Catherine Street Gang came to beat on Joe's stepbrother Pat Jr.—Joe fought them off alone. And that huge kid outside the vegetable market who called him a sissy for playing the violin. Joe never forgot that weird feeling when his right fist landed on the kid's chin—a crazy and sweet feeling at the same time. The big bully dropped like the onion sacks Joe used to lug through the market.

It was the very next day that Thurston had said, "You should come with me to the gym." They had never spoken much before.

It got colder with the darkness as they walked down some streets that were strange to Joe.

Even now, after several years, the city sometimes scared him. It was so big, with its own rules and codes. And there were so many people in the city, most of them as worried and hungry as his own family.

When the Barrows and Brookses came up

from the red-clay Buckalew Mountains in Alabama, where Joe was born on May 13, 1914, Detroit was the promised land. It seemed like everyone was heading north. There were jobs in the Ford plant that paid better than sharecropping; there was electricity and indoor plumbing in the apartment houses. Black people could start climbing the ladder just like whites. But now the jobs were disappearing and the bills were stacking up.

Life in a sharecropping family had been hard, too. Most of the sixteen children in the Barrow-Brooks clan worked the hard flaky soil sunup to sundown. But there were ponds to swim in and thick elms to scurry up. They played skin-the-tree and chased each other through the tangled branches. And there was always food, plenty of food, ham and corn and baked chicken legs and tomatoes and pork chops and cakes and . . .

The smells of Brewster's East Side Gymnasium were of sweat and ointment and the stink of bodies in action. Thurston waved to some friends while Joe took a long look around. Two boys sparred in an old canvas ring while an older man screamed at them from outside the ropes. Men pounded away on heavy bags while others peppered the speed bags with a machine-gun rhythm. Others skipped rope or stood on thin mats, stretching, or they hurled heavy leather medicine balls at each other. It was a whole new world in here, with its own drills and lessons. And it was as hot as Alabama in August.

He laid down Momma's fifty cents for a dented old locker, and when no one was looking, he shoved the violin case deep inside.

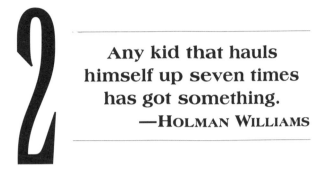

**Any kid that hauls
himself up seven times
has got something.**
      —HOLMAN WILLIAMS

When Joe came home from the gym one Saturday, he found Momma and the music teacher sitting together in the kitchen. They talked for a while. It was better this way, said the music teacher as he stood to go. Let the boy pursue his talents. Maybe it won't be boxing, but I can tell you it's not music. After he left, Joe and Momma sat in silence for a while.

As he often did, perhaps Joe started thinking about his natural father, Munroe Barrow, a big man, six feet two and strong but with something sad and broken in his face. Momma always said that Mun was a good man who had tried hard but couldn't take the pressure of hard times and a big family. All his dreams kept tumbling down. When Joe, the seventh child, was two years old, Mun was taken away to the Searcy Hospital for the Negro Insane.

Over the years he'd come home to visit his family, making jokes about how he had "escaped." All the brothers and sisters—Susie, Lonnie, Eulalia, Emarell, De Leon, Alvanius and Joseph Louis—would gather around this man who seemed more like a kindly uncle than a father, who loved them in a way they could not quite understand.

But they all understood their stepfather, Pat Sr., even though it was strange how Momma could love two men so different. Pat had eight children of his own but loved everyone fairly. He was everything Mun was not: tough and rational, with a faith in the small steps that could make things better. It was Pat who had brought them out of the mountains to Detroit, who made sure they all had a chance in these bad times. He and Momma had saved each other and their families.

"Momma," said Joe, "I know you and Pat don't want me to box, but I could be good."

"You do what you want, Joseph. But no

matter what you do, remember you're from a Christian family, and always act that way."

A few weeks later, Joe quit vocational school to devote all his time to training. It was up at dawn to run, a quick breakfast, then out into the streets for a day of odd jobs, mostly hauling crates. The evening belonged to his new friends—the heavy bag, the peanut bag, the jump rope and the medicine ball.

An older fighter named Holman Williams started watching Joe and offering tips. Soon he was training him every night, teaching him how to snap out the jab, how to feint, how to move after a punch, how to put his weight behind the hook. Boxing, Joe learned, was more like a chess match than a street fight. A boxer was respected for his brains, his ability to calculate an opponent's weaknesses, to exploit his mistakes. And there was so much to know—the geometry of the ring, the brutal physics of combination punches, the psychology of a fighter's will. Around the gym, old-timers sometimes called boxing "the sweet science."

And when the old-timers got to talking,

they'd surely talk about Jack Johnson, even pull out old magazines with his pictures. Those eyes, set deep in the dark handsome face, seemed on fire. That bald head, smooth and strong, and the tough jaw and rippling shoulders. He was the champ, the old-timers would say, until the white man stole his title.

No one could beat John Arthur Johnson, the master boxer who lived a reckless, high-style superstar life when blacks were supposed to remain ever humble. White America searched the land for a "Great White Hope," as sportswriters called him. An old champion came out of retirement just to beat Johnson, and was knocked out.

Johnson was hounded out of the country by laws that forbade sexual relationships between men and women of different races. Eventually he lost his title, and the white boxing world vowed that never again would a black man be its heavyweight champion.

The big sparring partner swung his left in a wide slow arc. Joe ducked and came up with a hard short right. The big man dropped, rolled

In 1915, the year after Joe Louis was born, a so-called "great white hope" named Jess Willard defeated Jack Johnson for the heavyweight title in Havana.

The image of Johnson—a cocky, powerful, flamboyant black man who refused to be subservient to whites—would haunt boxing for many years and affect Joe's life. Here, Johnson shows off his strength in what is also a symbolic pose. At the end of those ropes are horses pulling him in different directions, but he will not be moved.

over, moaned. Everyone in the gym started yelling. Joe whipped off his headgear, turned to Holman.

"I want a fight."

"You haven't sparred enough."

"I'm ready." Joe threw down his headgear and glared at Holman.

"Well, I guess we'll have to find out."

Johnny Miler helped him find out. Johnny Miler had slick hair, a nice smile. He looked easy to beat. In his autobiography, Joe remembered wishing that he was fighting this first fight under his real name, Joe Barrow, so everyone would know it when he beat Miler, a white ex-Olympic boxer. But it was too late to make a change. He would be fighting as Joe Louis, the name he had taken so Momma wouldn't find out too quick about his fights.

The lights were hot, and the jeers and drunken shouts of the crowd burned in Joe's ears as Johnny Miler waved to his fans each time he knocked Joe down. Joe could not feel his legs, and his arms were limp celery, but somehow he hoisted himself back up for the seventh time. Somehow he finished the round, made it back to the dressing room.

"Well," said Holman, "any kid that hauls himself up seven times has got something."

Back home Momma dabbed at his cuts with a hot cloth. He was glad now he hadn't used his real name. Momma knew, of course, but not too many other people.

"Well, you tried," said Pat Sr., folding the merchandise check into his pocket. "That's the end of that. I got you a job at the Ford plant."

3

A black fighter needs a black manager.
—JOHN ROXBOROUGH

Joe hated the job. He would later say he felt as if someone was sticking a knife in his back as he pushed each truck body up onto the conveyor belt. He was too tired and in too much pain to fall asleep when he got home. He didn't want to spend his life like this.

He went back to the gym.

First thing we are going to do, Holman told him, is teach you to keep your left up. That's why Miler kept putting you down.

He tied Joe's right hand to the ring post and sent his friend Thurston McKinney in to box Joe with two hands.

"Tie me loose!" Joe roared, trying to protect himself with his left as Thurston pummeled him

Joe's mom, Lillie Brooks, wasn't happy when he started boxing as a teenager, and she hated to see him fight, but once he started winning—without getting hurt—she would visit him in his training gym.

And she never stopped stuffing Joe and his brothers and sisters.

with hooks and crosses, but Holman and Atler Ellis, the old gym owner, just laughed. Joe would never forget this lesson. He'd always have his left up now, even at the breakfast table.

Another chance. Joe fought Otis Thomas at the Forest Athletic Club in Detroit, but Joe kept seeing Johnny Miler's face as he landed punch after punch. Midway through the first round, Otis Thomas lay slumped on the canvas.

Thirteen more went down, and Joe was an amateur boxing star. Each of the merchandise checks he gave to Momma and Pat bought the family groceries for a week. He was still fighting as Joe Louis; he couldn't change now that everyone knew who he was. Momma was proud. And there was even a skinny little neighborhood boy named Walker Smith who idolized Joe, followed him everywhere, carried his bag to the gym. When Walker moved to New York, he told Joe he was going to be a fighter, too. Joe laughed and wished him luck.

Joe began to travel for fights, to Chicago, Boston, and Toronto, mostly winning, making friends with other boxers along the way. Every city had its own brand of depression, unemployment and hungry young fighters.

One day a well-dressed man came by the Brewster gym to watch Joe train. Everyone started whispering. Thurston gave Joe the thumbs-up sign. This was a good thing.

John Roxborough was a neighborhood hero, a smart black man who had made a fortune buying and selling real estate and running a "numbers bank," the control center of an illegal lottery. Few people in the community thought of Roxborough as a criminal. Most saw him as a shrewd, cultivated man who would have been a real banker if he had been born white. Some people felt the same way thirty years later when another black "numbers banker," Don King, became an important fight promoter for Muhammad Ali and others.

A few weeks later Roxborough watched Joe lose a tough fight to another black heavyweight and invited him to his office, a bare front room with a few old desks and chairs, a single secretary typing a letter in the corner. But in the back, phones rang and men shouted. That was the office where the numbers bets were taken. Roxborough told Joe to take a seat.

Roxborough told Joe that a black fighter needed a black manager, someone who cared about him, looked out for him, made sure he didn't get used up before his prime. Later, Joe would say in his autobiography that he sensed his life was about to take another good turn.

Roxborough offered Joe a fifty-fifty split—they would share Joe's fight purses after he turned pro. Roxborough would pay all expenses from his half. It was a generous offer. Joe agreed. Meanwhile Roxborough gave Joe some spending money and free credit at the drugstore for bandages and rubbing alcohol.

One night he invited Joe to dinner. The house was huge and beautiful. Everyone was dressed like the elegant people in magazines. Joe had never seen black people living like this. He remembered Thurston telling him a champion could become a millionaire.

Joe started to wolf down the food on his plate, but Roxborough's sharp look seemed to tell him, Slow down. If you listen to me, soon you'll have plenty of everything.

4

**The heavyweight
division for a Negro ain't
likely. But if you really
ain't gonna be another
Jack Johnson you got
some hope.**

—JACK BLACKBURN

Joe never forgot his early impressions of Jack Blackburn, his most important trainer. Bloodshot eyes stared out of a dark, scarred face. A bullet head shone under the naked bulbs that hung from the ceiling of his Chicago gym. The voice rasped, "Plant your feet more. Get power comin' up your legs."

At first, Jack Blackburn scared Joe. He had fought a hundred times as a lightweight and done prison time for murder. But when Roxborough had sent Joe off to Chicago, he had said Blackburn was the best

"You know, boy," said Blackburn, "the heavyweight division for a Negro ain't likely. But if you really ain't gonna be another Jack

Johnson you got some hope. You got to listen to everything I say. Jump when I say jump, sleep when I say sleep. Other than that, you're wasting my time."

"I promise," said Joe.

Blackburn nodded. "Okay, Chappie."

"Okay, Chappie," Joe replied.

Blackburn grinned. That would be their nickname for each other from now on.

Chappie, John Roxborough and Julien Black, Joe's other manager, laid down rules for Joe.

If he really wanted a crack at the title someday, they told him, he had to avoid reminding people of Jack Johnson. He must never go into a nightclub alone, never have his picture taken with a white woman, and never, ever, smile when he knocked out a white fighter.

They made it clear that Joe was not supposed to play the stereotype of the shuffling, servile Negro, either, but to be reserved, friendly and dignified. They always had to be on guard against the boxing establishment and the white press.

Chappie laid it out in his own language,

according to Joe's book, reminding him of the "little black toy dolls . . . with thick red lips. They looked foolish. I got the message—don't look like a fool nigger doll. Look like a black man with dignity."

It was a lot of pressure for a young fighter. These men were putting their trust in Joe. He set his face in a sullen-eyed mask. It would be his trademark expression. Only his friends would see him laugh.

Julien Black put Joe up in a nice apartment near the gym. Downstairs lived Bill Bottoms, who would be his camp cook and lifelong friend. Most days started at six A.M. with roadwork, then back to the apartment for a short nap and breakfast.

The rest of the day was spent at the gym, where Chappie passed on a lifetime of boxing knowledge. Turn your fist as your punch makes contact. Hook over the jab. Never cross your feet as you move sideways. Don't bother head-hunting—kill the body and the head will die.

Sometimes Roxborough would visit and teach Joe, too. He took him out to restaurants

Harlem was a center of hip entertainment for whites as well as blacks in the 1930's. This is a scene at one of the most famous night spots, the Cotton Club.

and showed him the art of fine dining, and bought him suits, stylish but conservative, like his own.

They knew that Joe was special, that he had something beyond talent: He had a knockout punch. That meant more than victory. That meant box-office popularity. People want to see the knockout, Chappie told him.

But it meant even more than that for a black fighter then. "You have to go for the knockout," warned Chappie. "Negro fighters do not go to town winning decisions."

Joe's first pro fight was on July 4, 1934, against Jack Kracken, Chicago's top white heavyweight.

Kracken was older, stronger and more experienced, but when the bell rang Joe went out and banged at Kracken's ribs until he lowered his guard. "Kill the body and the head will die!" yelled Chappie.

Joe dropped him with a left to the chin. Kracken could not get up. The fight was over in less than two minutes.

"You looked sluggish out there," snarled Chappie. "You follow the diet I gave you?"

"'Cept for the dozen bananas I ate before the fight."

Nobody thought it was funny.

Joe sent most of the prize money home and kept the rest to celebrate with Freddie Guinyard, his old Detroit neighborhood pal. They devoted a day to their favorite vices: bowling and junk food.

Joe won three of his first four fights by quick knockouts. He was undefeated and on the rise.

One day Joe noticed some tough-looking white guys lurking in a corner of the gym—gangsters who scared fighters into losing on purpose so they could bet against them. Chappie chased them off, then grabbed Joe's arm.

"Listen here, Chappie," said Blackburn, "you better not ever throw a fight. 'Cause I'll know. And then it'll be me and you." Blackburn was only half Joe's size, but he meant it. Once, twenty years ago, he'd beat up Jack Johnson in a sparring match.

Joe had no interest in losing on purpose. The pay was too good for winning. He wanted to be a champion, not an opponent, a punching bag, a mob stooge. The boxing world was full of criminals, but there had to be a clean way, too.

The knockouts kept coming and the press followed. Couldn't open a sports page without seeing his picture, usually glaring out, that sullen-faced mask so people wouldn't think he was like Jack Johnson. People traveled across

Chicago to watch him train.

One afternoon Joe turned around in the middle of a sparring session and saw a beautiful, well-dressed young woman watching him from the crowd. He caught a left on the cheek while he was watching her.

Her name was Marva Trotter. She was eighteen, smart and ambitious. She was studying clothing design. Soon they would be in love.

5

I should be doing
this to you.
—PRIMO CARNERA

Lee Ramage. Hans Birkie. Stanley Poreda. Joe
was knocking out top heavyweights and making
good money for those days, sometimes six thousand dollars a fight. He was ready for the
big-time glamour matches in New York. But
Chappie explained that New York was not quite
ready for Joe.

The group that owned the main fight arena,
Madison Square Garden, also had a monopoly
on the heavyweight title. Nobody got to fight
for the title without their approval. They told
Roxborough that because Joe was "colored," he
would have to lose a few to the fighters they
controlled. Otherwise, Joe would not fight in
New York.

Okay, said Roxborough. Joe won't fight in New York.

It was a bold stand, but Roxborough, like everyone else around Joe, believed he was more than a fighter. They saw someone who could help make changes and give other people the strength to do the same. There were times when even Joe sensed this power.

It was different from the usual adulation, the fans on their feet screaming for another quick kill, the women throwing themselves at him (he did not always resist) or the frenzied press coining his many nicknames. Most of them were silly, a few insulting, and only one really stuck-- the Brown Bomber.

He sensed this power in the street. Black people were hailing him on corners, at restaurants and barbershops and gas stations, pumping a fist in the air, saying things like "Way to go, Brown Bomber, show the white man who we are!"

Joe was barely twenty years old, not even a top contender, but Joe Louis the symbol was already Number One. Sometimes it felt like a terrible burden and sometimes it felt like an amazing gift. Later, he would see it was both.

"You see, there's a silent agreement never to
have another Negro champion." The little white
man mashed out his cigar and looked up at Joe,
Chappie and Roxborough as they leaned in
closer around their small table at the Frog Club,
a "colored" nightspot. "Look at Jack Dempsey—
he dodged Harry Wills for years because he was
black. But we're gonna change all that."

Mike Jacobs was white and a promoter, but
he was an outsider, too, as far as the boxing
establishment was concerned. Wily and tough,
Jacobs grew up in New York, a Jew in a poor
Irish neighborhood. Early success scalping opera
and boxing tickets helped him work his way into
the fight world. Now he had put together his
own organization to take on the big boys in
New York.

"You're all colored," he said, "and I'm a
Jew. It's going to be hard for us to do anything.
But if you stick with me, I think we can do it."

The key was the Hearst Milk Fund, a charity
that took a cut from the fight proceeds at the
Garden to feed hungry children. When the Gar-

den monopoly reduced the amount of money that could be given to the Fund, Mr. Hearst himself became enraged. This was William Randolph Hearst, the publisher of a chain of newspapers and one of the most powerful men in the country. Mike Jacobs let him know that the Milk Fund would get even more money than before if he were running boxing. Suddenly sportswriters on Hearst's papers began to drum up attention for Jacobs and Joe. Soon it would be time to strike.

Meanwhile, Joe was spending more and more time with Marva Trotter, but he never got to be alone with her. She was always bringing a sister along, or making him take her to see his mother. Marva and Momma clicked right away, like they knew something he didn't.

Joe was torn. He liked the idea of a life with Marva, but he also liked to cruise around the neighborhood in his brand-new Buick with his old pal Freddie, picking up girls.

He was too busy to think about it much. After several more knockouts Joe began training for Primo Carnera, a former heavyweight champion. Carnera was no master boxer, but he was a giant for his times—6 feet 5 inches, 260 pounds—and he could hit. Chappie hired the biggest sparring partners he could find so Joe could practice slipping their hooks and moving inside their long reaches where he could pound the body until the head died.

The fight was set for June 25, 1935, at Yankee Stadium in New York, and as the date drew close a fierce controversy arose. Mussolini, the fascist dictator of Italy, who would later fight on Hitler's side in World War II, had invaded Ethiopia, a small East African nation with a rich ancient heritage but few modern weapons. Some of the Ethiopian soldiers met the advancing Italian army with nothing but spears.

Many people in America were outraged. Petitions were passed to cancel the match as a protest against the invasion. Sportswriters began to frame the Carnera-Louis fight as a metaphor for a big Italian bully attacking a smaller darker man. It would not be the last time a Joe Louis fight was used to symbolize a larger conflict. Joe tried to ignore it and concentrate on Carnera.

But a less-publicized controversy arose that Joe refused to ignore. The boxing establishment refused to give black reporters the same ringside working-press seats they routinely gave to white reporters. The official explanation was that those seats were reserved for daily newspapers— and almost all the black newspapers were weekly papers. Joe joined some black and white writers to make a public protest. For the first time, the black reporters got their fair share of seats.

Joe was beginning to get a sense of his power to do good, and people began to look to him more and more to take on opponents outside the ring.

But first he had to win inside the ring. Later, Joe remembered feeling nervous as he stepped into the ring and shook his arms loose under his blue-and-red robe. Chappie reminded him to go for the body first, then the head.

Joe looked over at Carnera. The giant was sweating hard under the lights.

The referee called them out for instructions, then sent them back to their corners. It was taking forever. Chappie was still talking, but Joe tuned him out. He just wanted the bell to ring so he could land his first punch and chase the butterflies in his gut.

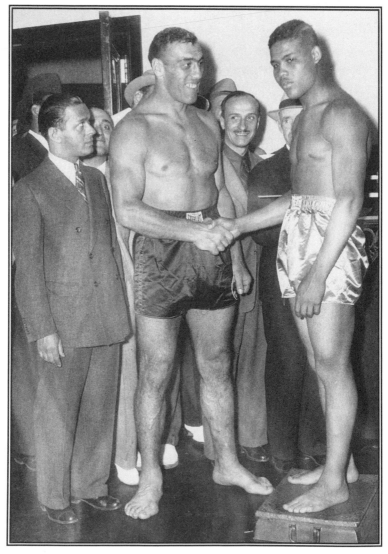

Primo Carnera was 6 feet 5 inches tall, 4 inches taller than Joe, and, at 260, some 65 pounds heavier when they fought in 1935. But the wrong man is smiling at this prefight weigh-in. Joe proved that the bigger they are, the harder they fall.

Joe stalked out of the corner, and from that first punch the fight was his. It took a while to get used to Carnera's size and his awkward style, but the giant was powerless to stop Joe from slipping his long punches and working inside. He battered Carnera with short, chopping punches. Carnera was hurt and flustered.

Carnera tried to wrap up Joe and smother him with his bulk, but Joe actually picked Carnera up off his feet and drove him into the ropes. Joe remembered hearing Carnera say, "I should be doing this to you."

It was over by the fifth round. Joe put Carnera down three times with hard crosses. The third time, Carnera, dazed, his mouth pooled in blood, could not get up.

6

I don't like
watermelon.
—JOE LOUIS

The preacher's deep voice rumbled through the church. Joe would remember his words all his life. God gives a few of us special gifts, the preacher said, and to one man sitting right here he has given a powerful talent in boxing, a gift to uplift the spirit of the Negro race.

The congregation rocked to the words and craned to catch a glimpse of the smiling woman and the strong young man in the center pew, Lillie Barrow Brooks and her boy. Joe later said that he kept cool but felt a jolt inside when the preacher called him one of the "chosen."

Out on the street, people called to him, cheered.

Joe was in training for Kingfish Levinsky, a

ferocious puncher who would test him, or so the reporters claimed. Everyone was worried whether or not Joe could take a punch. Joe was worried about something else. Chappie was drinking too much. He warned him to slow down—he was damaging his health.

"Mind your own business," Chappie would growl, disappearing into his room for the night.

Joe later admitted feeling foolish telling Chappie how to live his life. Before Joe was born, the man was scrapping out a fighter's living in dusty towns across America.

But now here they were in the car on the way to the fight, and Chappie was hunched over in pain, trying to breathe.

"Listen to me, Chappie," said Joe. "If I knock out Levinsky in one round, will you quit drinking for six months?"

Chappie flashed his strange little grin. Levinsky was tough. "Sure thing, Chappie."

Halfway through the first round Levinsky was down on the canvas, tangled in the ropes, screaming at the referee not to let Joe hit him again.

Back in the dressing room Joe felt a tap on

the shoulder. "You're gonna let me out of this thing, right, Chappie?"

Everyone knew the Max Baer fight was the next big step. Baer had beaten Carnera a few years before for the heavyweight title but then lost it to the current champion, James Braddock, the "Cinderella Man," in a shocking upset.

While he was champion, Baer had milked the title for all the glamour it was worth. Big and handsome, Baer could fight, but he was even better as the charming party guest or the Great Lover. Now, with his popularity in decline, he was desperate for his title back. He knew his only way to get another shot at Braddock was by beating Joe Louis.

Joe trained hard but something was wrong: no rhythm in his moves, no groove. Sparring partners found his chin. The speed bag refused to chatter.

He was missing Marva. He never knew when he was going to get a chance to see her next, to talk, to be alone with her. Julien Black sensed trouble and took Joe by the arm. He told Joe to

Joe and his wife, the former Marva Trotter, were one of the hottest couples in Harlem in the 1930's.

marry Marva. He called her the next day and she said yes.

This time, 95,000 people jammed into Yankee Stadium. Joe looked across the ring at Baer and his celebrity cornerman, the legendary former champion Jack Dempsey.

But nothing was scaring Joe tonight, not the crowd, not Baer's bone-crushing right, not the pressure of the fight. Joe looked down at ringside and saw Marva. She seemed to glow. Just a few hours earlier they had stood together in a large apartment in Harlem and become husband and wife.

The bell rang and Joe met Baer in the middle of the ring. Joe threw a hard uppercut and Baer shook. Baer looked tight and timid. Joe looked fast and strong. He threw fluid combinations and waited for openings. Baer was bleeding, confused.

Joe finished it in the fourth round with a left hook and a right to the head. Baer crumpled to the canvas for the third and last time.

The crowd went crazy. Even Chappie

smiled. It seemed truly possible now that Joe could be champion.

The day after the fight Baer said some nasty things to the press about how Joe was lucky and did not really deserve to be in the ring with him. Max Baer's quotes were not the only words that bothered Joe. He was noticing the way the press described him, even in praise.

The New York *Sun,* the same paper that forty years earlier had warned of the humiliation of having a black champion, wrote in 1935 that Joe had "the skill, strength and courage of which champions are made." That was good. But the editorial also stated the "American Negro is a natural athlete. The generations of toil in the cotton fields have not obliterated the strength and grace of the African native."

It was as if Joe had not trained hard to hone his skill. And the editorial suggested that his managers wanted him to be "a credit to his race." What did that mean?

In other stories, a phrase like "born killer" would pop up.

A writer would note Joe's "cold stare" or

There were other black sports heroes in Joe's time, some of them better known to African Americans than to whites. Satchel Paige was the pitching star of the Negro Leagues, a thriving baseball circuit in the days when black players were barred from the major leagues.

liken his ring style to that of a "jungle beast."

Joe knew those were ways of saying he was less than human, of calling him an animal. It made him angry. Years later, he would come to understand that many whites in America could not bear to see a powerful, successful black man. They felt threatened, and found comfort in thinking of him as a natural killer sprung from the wilderness.

But Joe began to realize that all the love and support he was getting from black people across the country, the letters and telegrams and shouts on the street, were not just about his knockouts. People saw that Joe had an opportunity to help change the way blacks were represented in white newspapers, books, movies, magazines, in white culture at large. And he was representing them all.

Once, a white photographer became annoyed when Joe refused to pose for a picture with a watermelon in his hand, a stereotypical photograph in those days, the "happy darky" picture. He lied and said, "I don't like watermelon."

The image of Jack Johnson kept flashing in his mind; Joe had to be reserved, friendly and dignified.

Meanwhile, Joe continued to unwind from the Baer fight, and to adjust to his life with Marva. A friend introduced him to a new passion, golf, and Joe spent sweet, lazy days on the greens.

And somewhere in the middle of the Atlantic Ocean, an ex-champion from Germany stood on the deck of a steamship and dreamed of winning his title back.

To do that, he would have to knock out this Joe Louis.

7

Joe's life became a party. He was twenty-two years old, rich and handsome and famous. Unbeaten in twenty-seven professional fights. He ran with the black superstars of his time, Duke Ellington, the great jazz composer; Bill "Bojangles" Robinson, the dancer and Hollywood star; the singer Lena Horne; and Paul Robeson, one of America's greatest opera singers and a fighter for human rights. It didn't seem as though he had time to train much these days, and when he did show up at camp, he brought his golf clubs along, which made Chappie mad.

It was not just a matter of proper attitude as far as Chappie was concerned, although it was true that Max Schmeling was dangerous and

Paul Robeson was an All-American football player before he went on to become a famous political activist and one of the world's greatest singers. This is from his 1933 movie The Emperor Jones. *In 1940, he recorded a song, "King Joe," about Joe Louis, lyrics by Richard Wright, music by Count Basie.*

that Joe needed to concentrate if he wanted to beat him and then get a shot at Braddock's title.

But the body has its own circuits of memory, and Chappie worried that Joe's body might get confused. A golf swing and a punch are two very different motions. And Joe seemed to take it all so lightly.

Max Schmeling was not taking it all lightly.

"I've seen him spar," Schmeling told reporters. "I know how to beat him."

Nobody really believed Schmeling, but the promotors were glad he was making a good show for ticket sales. It had been more than four years since Schmeling won the title on a foul— Jack Sharkey punched him below the belt. Two years later, Sharkey won it back. Since then, Schmeling had knocked out a string of contenders, working his way up to Joe. But as their fight neared, the events of the outside world began to pierce the sports-world bubble.

It was 1936. Adolf Hitler and his Nazis had seized control of Germany, Schmeling's homeland. The Nazis believed in the superiority of the "Aryan" race, and their bigotry and hatred had already taken root in many German people.

Jews, Gypsies, people of color, homosexuals, trade unionists, political activists and just about anyone else who failed to meet the Nazi regime's requirements for the Master Race, which included tape measurements of the head and face, were terrorized and sometimes killed. Anyone who protested the intolerance (and some Germans did) was also destroyed.

Soon, Germany's military aggression would trigger World War II, but this was a time of great tension as the rest of Europe and the United States held its breath and wished—or pretended—that the Nazis would go away. Though the true horrors of Nazi Germany, such as the murderous concentration camps, would not be revealed for several years, people were upset.

American Jews circulated petitions to stop the fight, maintaining that it was wrong to allow this sporting event to take place as if nothing was happening in Germany. Joe understood the point—he'd been through something similar over Ethiopia before the Carnera fight—but he thought it was being blown out of proportion.

Max Schmeling was not a Nazi. Schmeling felt cheated, in fact, to be caught in the crossfire of such an international controversy. He considered himself a professional athlete, a boxer, and all he wanted was his championship back.

In fact, Hitler had let it be known that he did not want Schmeling to fight Joe Louis. He was afraid Louis would win, as most fans and experts predicted, and that if the world saw a black man whip a true German, Hitler's racial theories would look foolish.

While they apparently understood the politics of the situation, it seemed as though neither Schmeling nor Joe really cared. All either of them wanted to do was fight and win.

A rain delay pushed the bout back a day, but they finally fought on the damp night of June 19, 1936. There were 40,000 people in the stands of Yankee Stadium, and they all seemed to be rooting for Joe, along with Momma, Marva and Freddie Guinyard. Joe's brothers and sisters were there, and rows of old friends from Detroit. Many of them were thinking beyond this fight. After Joe beat Schmeling, there would be no way that the champion, Jim Braddock, could duck Joe. He was just a few punches away from becoming the champ.

Joe let his robe slip away. He shook his arms

loose. Chappie's bony fingers kneaded his neck. "Don't go for the knockout yet, keep your left high."

Joe told Chappie not to worry, that Schmeling was a "pushover."

At the bell, Schmeling waded out in a tight crouch, almost doubled over. Joe moved around him, popping his long jab down into Schmeling's eye, which soon swelled shut.

The second round was like the first, with Schmeling getting tagged but staying down in his crouch. Joe dipped down to throw a left hook. Chappie had warned him to keep his left up, but Joe felt confident. The hook landed.

So did Schmeling's counterpunch, a blistering right cross. Joe went reeling. It would not be the last time.

They fought hard for several rounds but Joe grew flustered. His uppercuts bounced off Schmeling's rock-hard ribs. Even when his crosses landed cleanly, they seemed futile. It was like punching the side of a bus.

And Schmeling's rights kept looping in again and again, crashing into Joe's head like some mechanical bludgeon, coming in harder and faster each time.

Then Joe went down. He sprang right up, but in a way the fight was over. He had never been down as a pro, never been hurt like this. Even as he held on for another eight rounds, Joe was already gone. Dazed and battered, he took punch after punch as Americans hunched beside their radios, winced and screamed with each Schmeling bomb as if they were getting hit, too.

"Don't kill my boy, Dear Lord!" Momma screamed as Freddie Guinyard carried her out of the stadium.

Chappie clutched the towel, terrified but true to his promise to Joe not to throw it into the ring and stop the fight.

Schmeling's relentless beating was actually holding Joe up, but finally, near the end of the twelfth, Schmeling stepped back. Joe Louis, once undefeated and now almost unconscious, toppled to the canvas.

A few hours later Joe called Momma to tell her he was okay. If she had seen his face, puffed out

Max Schmeling and his wife, the actress Annie Oudra, are welcomed by Adolf Hitler after Max beat Joe Louis. But Max was never a Nazi. He and Joe were friendly after the war.

like a bruised peach, she might not have believed him.

"I was sitting on the dressing table and crying like I don't think I ever did before," he said in his autobiography. "It seemed at that moment I would just die."

He was not the only one who cried that night. Americans found out how important Joe had become to some of them. Brokenhearted people sat numb beside their radios and wandered silent into the streets. Men stoned streetcars in Chicago. A girl in New York drank a bottle of poison and almost died.

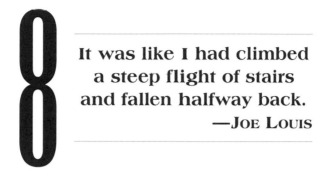

**It was like I had climbed
a steep flight of stairs
and fallen halfway back.**

—JOE LOUIS

A lucky punch, Roxborough told the reporters, and drove Joe back to that fancy apartment in Harlem. But there were no movie stars, no jazzmen, no party girls waving bottles of champagne. For days it was just Joe and Marva hiding from the world.

It's hard now to realize how important this twenty-two-year-old boxer had become as a symbol for black Americans. He had risen to the top of an old slave sport and made himself his own master. He was even managed and trained by black men!

Of course, he was, after all, just a boxer, and there were brilliant black poets like Langston Hughes; scientists like Dr. Charles Drew, who developed the medical use of blood plasma; novelists like Richard Wright; and politicians like Adam Clayton Powell, Jr., as well as lawyers, artists, businesspeople, educators. But none of them was as well known in the white community as Joe.

It was Powell who wrote, in the weekly New York *Amsterdam News*, after the loss to Schmeling: ". . . along came the Brown Bomber, Death in the Evening, and our racial morale took a sky high leap. . . . Then . . . the Yankee Stadium fiasco. . . . Gone today is the jauntiness, the careless abandon, the spring in our stride— we're just shufflin' along."

Joe was out there representing all black people in those bitter days when most colleges admitted few if any blacks, when college-educated blacks were lucky to get jobs as railroad waiters, when even the Army was segregated. There were no blacks in major-league baseball. In movies they mostly played servants.

And there was Joe, a symbol of pride, a hope for a future in which discrimination would be knocked out, in which there would be justice and equality for everyone.

When he lost to Schmeling, his very first pro defeat, some of that hope was beaten down, too.

It was a lot to pile on the shoulders of a twenty-two-year-old boxer, but people were desperate.

No wonder Joe and Marva hid away in the apartment.

The papers carried news of Schmeling's glorious homecoming, the medals pinned to his chest, the intimate dinner with Hitler. Films of the fight played to sold-out crowds in Germany. That summer of 1936, Berlin was the host of the Olympics. Hitler sank millions into stadiums and facilities, eager to unveil his twisted vision to the world through parades and pomp. Max Schmeling's unexpected knockout now seemed like destiny.

The American hero of the so-called Nazi Olympics was Jesse Owens, a twenty-two-year-old black runner and long-jumper who won four gold medals. In the United States, he was hailed as proof that Hitler's theories were absurd, that the Nazis were really not such a threat. It was

1936 was a big sports year for Germany. The so-called Nazi Olympics, in Berlin, were a great success. While Jesse Owens salutes the American flag after winning one of his four gold medals, the second-place finisher in the broad jump, Lutz Long, gives the Nazi salute.

more pretending; the German armies were poised for their triumphant march through Europe.

As Jesse Owens's star rose, Joe's was falling. Back in America, nobody was ready to forgive Joe.

On the street, people shouted, "There's the money!" when Chappie arrived at the apartment with Joe's equipment bag. Unwilling to believe he could actually lose, many black fans preferred to believe that Joe had thrown the fight for money. A few even claimed he had been kidnapped hours before the opening bell and forced to take a drug that slowed his reflexes.

But after a few weeks, the nation returned to greater concerns, such as the depression at home and the threat of war in Europe.

Joe was at his lowest point. "It was like I had climbed a steep flight of stairs and fallen halfway back," Joe later wrote in his autobiography.

He began to train again in a cold fever. He had to study every nuance of his style, destroy every bad habit. He was starting up the stairs again.

Jack Sharkey was another ex-champion, a brawler with a knack for publicity. No colored fighter can beat me, he told the press before his fight with Joe. Once, that would have angered

Joe, but now he saw it for what it was, just a cheap stunt to jack up ticket sales.

Besides, Joe was in another state of mind, beyond responding to the glare of the press and public. By the time he got into the ring with Sharkey, he was in what athletes call "the zone": all reality disappears except the one task at hand.

Sharkey lay unconscious by the third round, blood seeping from his mouth. Joe looked down and thought about Schmeling. Al Ettore and Eddie Sims were next, and they were just stepping stones to Schmeling, too. It did not matter whom Joe knocked out. Until he fought the German again, they were all just preludes to Schmeling.

Mike Jacobs was still hustling. The politics of the boxing world were getting more confused every day. Braddock was waiting to see who would offer him the most money for a shot at his title. Schmeling wanted that shot and everyone knew he deserved it, but U.S. promoters didn't want to risk losing the title to a foreign country, least of all Nazi Germany.

Suddenly the idea of a black man as heavy-weight champion was not so terrifying. At least all the money that went along with a champion's reign—the promotion fees, leases, stadium rents and advertising—would stay in the United States.

So the white moneymen took another look at Joe Louis and realized what a "model Negro" he was. He had never dated a white woman (in public), never gloated when he knocked a white man out. This was no Jack Johnson.

Roxborough's lessons had paid off. The contracts were drawn up, the date was set: June 22, 1937.

James Braddock was tough and savvy, but he never had a chance against the hailstorm of blinding punches that overwhelmed him. He tried Schmeling's strategy, crouching to lure Joe into dropping his left. But Joe never dropped his left.

People always talked about Joe's right hand, the thunderous right cross, but Joe thought his left was just as good. The big secret was in combinations, jabs and hooks and crosses and uppercuts thrown in various sequences. Most of the time the fighter who loses is the one who gets figured out, whose strategies become predictable.

Joe's other secret was less complicated. Even he was not exactly sure why, but for some reason he needed very little space to throw a knockout punch. Other fighters wound up, telegraphed the blow, but Joe could hit hard from any angle, even when he was crowded all the way inside.

Tonight Chappie leaned back and enjoyed the show. He had taken talent and turned it into flawless craft. But when the eighth round started, Joe grew impatient with the subtleties of boxing. He called on an old punch he had learned in those first hard days in Detroit, the D.O.A., Dead On your Ass, a crude haymaker that never failed. Braddock went down to stay. Later, Braddock would say, "When you're hit by Louis it's like a light bulb breaking in your face."

A credit to his race
—the human race.
—JIMMY CANNON

"Champion of the world. A Black boy. Some Black mother's son. He was the strongest man in the world. People drank Coca-Colas like ambrosia and ate candy bars like Christmas," wrote Maya Angelou in *I Know Why the Caged Bird Sings*. She was recalling a childhood night with friends and family in a tiny store in Arkansas as the radio broadcast the Louis knockout.

"Those who lived too far had made arrangements to stay in town. It wouldn't do for a Black man and his family to be caught on a lonely country road on a night when Joe Louis had proved that we were the strongest people in the world."

Cities and towns exploded with joy. African Americans took to the streets and the rooftops and the fields shouting his name.

Whatever else happens, tonight the heavyweight champion of the world is one of us.

No one pretended that suddenly, like magic, hate and poverty would be gone. President Roosevelt's New Deal, a huge program to create jobs and save big business, was nudging America out of the depression in 1937, but blacks would be among the last to be helped. Yet blacks were inspired by Joe.

One of us is making it. It's possible.

John Thompson, the Georgetown University basketball coach, lived with his parents in the basement of the house his mother cleaned for a white family. The Thompsons were invited upstairs to hear the fight.

"When Joe knocked the fighter out, however, the people jumped up and turned the radio off," reported Thompson in a book by Joe Louis's son. "So my mother and father quickly said good night and went downstairs. The minute they got downstairs they yelled like hell in celebration of the win."

For Joe, the days after he won the title were a haze of applause, parties, telegrams, gifts and offers to be in movies, on stage, to *referee* fights for a thousand dollars, an enormous fee in those days.

"Life was beautiful," he wrote in his autobiography, "but then I got a real shocker: Some social workers from Lafayette, Alabama, got in touch with me. They told me my father, Munroe Barrow, was [still alive]. . . . I hate to say this, but it didn't mean too much to me."

Joe sent money to Alabama for his biological father's care, but never visited him. As far as he was concerned, Pat Brooks, Sr., who had died in 1936, was his real father.

Max Schmeling came back to the United States for the title he claimed he deserved.

Before the contracts were even signed, protests erupted and petitions began to spread. Jewish groups in America once again wanted the fight stopped in light of the mounting horrors in Europe. By now, 1938, many people knew that the Nazi war machine was poised to roll and that terror and death had become routine in Germany.

The promotors of the fight argued that despite all the conflict this was just a contest between two athletes: Schmeling wanted the title, Joe wanted revenge and everybody wanted to make some money.

But the idea of a fight free of politics was pure fantasy. The moment the match was announced, Joe Louis and Max Schmeling the boxers vanished. Two symbols took their place.

Max had gotten a hero's send-off in Germany, which included a meeting with Adolf Hitler. Therefore, Max Schmeling *was* Nazi Germany, the looming threat of death and fascism.

Joe had a meeting with President Roosevelt, who told him: "Joe, we're depending on those muscles for America." Therefore Joe was the only man who could stop Schmeling and save democracy.

Never have two people competed under such intense pressure. Joe already knew about the joy sports could bring to people's lives. Now he was seeing the dark side. In the weeks before the fight, American Nazis, in uniform, harrassed Joe at his training camp. Even Max, caught up in the fever of hype, made some racist comments about Joe.

Years later, it would be learned that not only had Schmeling been privately anti-Nazi, but he had hidden the children of a Jewish friend during an early attack on Jews in Germany.

Just before the second Schmeling fight, President Franklin D. Roosevelt invited Joe to the White House, squeezed his arm, and said, "We need muscles like yours to beat Germany."

Nevertheless, the world seemed poised for the outcome of Louis–Schmeling II. The lines were drawn, and whichever side won would own a powerful symbol of its beliefs. When the lights blazed on at Yankee Stadium that night of June 22, 1938, everyone expected to see an epic duel.

What they saw was a vicious beating that lasted little more than two minutes. Schmeling got only two punches off before Joe swarmed all over him. Joe fired a barrage of combinations, and within seconds Schmeling was helpless, clinging to the ropes while Joe hammered him to the canvas.

Schmeling went down, got up, and went down again. His manager threw in the towel but the referee ignored it.

Two hooks and a classic Joe Louis right to the jaw ended it. Schmeling lay broken. Joe stood in a neutral corner, his body quaking with adrenaline. This time, when the bars and houses emptied, the streets teemed with whites as well as blacks, with Americans of every color and ancestry.

Joe had crossed the line from superstar to living monument. A famous sportswriter named

Joe waited two years for his rematch with Max, then took exactly two minutes and four seconds to knock him out.

Jimmy Cannon wrote a line that might seem obvious today, but which caught the new mood: "Joe Louis is a credit to his race—the human race."

*

People often remember World War II as the "Good War." Three years after Schmeling went down, Japan bombed Pearl Harbor and the United States joined the fight against Hitler and his allies, Italy and Japan. In this war, unlike those that followed, most Americans were eager to take part, even though there was no end in sight.

Joe's reign as heavyweight champion seemed endless, too. Contenders rose through the ranks only to meet Joe and go tumbling back down. He fought so often and won so easily, sportswriters called his bouts "The Bum-of-the-Month Club."

Billy Conn was an exception. The former light-heavyweight champion from Pittsburgh outwitted Joe for twelve rounds, landing quick combinations and dancing away. It was an exciting fight people still talk about, but in the thirteenth round Conn tried to prove he could slug it out and Joe demolished him. They remained friendly in later years and often joked about how Conn had been champion for twelve rounds.

Around this time Joe got some very bad advice from an accountant who told him not to pay all the taxes he owed on his fight purses. The accountant assured Joe he could pay them later, and pay less.

It turned out to be a disaster, but Joe was at fault, too. He never saved any money, and he spent wildly on parties and pals. Although he and Marva had two children, he was rarely at home. Eventually his marriage broke up. He would marry twice more and be in debt for the rest of his life.

But the party ended, for a few years, in January 1942, when Joe joined the crowd and enlisted in the Army.

The way I carried myself during that comin' up made some whites begin to look at colored people different.
—JOE LOUIS

Obviously no one expected Joe to serve as a regular soldier. The Army was not interested in risking the heavyweight champion on the front lines. His assignment was to crisscross the country on morale-boosting tours, giving talks and fighting exhibition matches. Joe donated the purses from his last two civilian fights to the Naval Relief Fund, a generous gesture that further deepened his financial problems.

But no one knew then about his troubles; America saw only a hero. Newsreels showed him dining in the mess hall with the other soldiers, and his picture loomed from recruitment posters. He even predicted an early knockout of the enemy because "we're on God's side." That

It was in his private's uniform that Joe made the most famous prediction of World War II: "We will win because we're on God's side."

became a slogan of the war.

He may have also found ways of changing the Army he was promoting.

A story goes that as the press corps was leaving Camp Upton in New York after Joe's induction into the Army, the champion turned to a reporter he knew and gestured at the the black-only barracks of the segregated camp. "This is the real battle," said Joe.

Later, at Fort Riley, Kansas, Joe met a young black who had been a star athlete at the University of California at Los Angeles. His name was Jackie Robinson. The two became friends and together confronted the outright racism in the U.S. Army. First, Joe helped Robinson break the color bar of the segregated camp baseball team. It was a prelude for Robinson's greatest individual battle—breaking major league baseball's color barrier in 1947. Joe also called officials he knew in Washington, D.C., and helped Robinson and other young black soldiers go to Officer Candidate School.

Years later, Joe admitted that he came to resent the way the Army used his name for various projects while his fellow black soldiers were

Joe met Jackie Robinson in the Army and helped the fiery young lieutenant through some rough times. They posed for this picture right after the war, a year before Jackie became the first modern African American major league baseball player.

so badly discriminated against. Stories began to travel up from training camps in the Deep South, where black soldiers were beaten and killed just for entering white towns. There were painful memories of hearing ugly slurs from white officers and watching Nazi prisoners of war eat better food than American black soldiers did.

Joe never got much credit for his efforts. Years later, some blacks criticized him for his lack of high-profile participation in the civil rights movement of the sixties. But black soldiers and their families remembered that when Jackie Robinson joined the Brooklyn Dodgers, people said, "No Joe Louis, no Jackie Robinson."

Joe resumed boxing after the war and defended his title against all comers, including Max Baer's brother Buddy and Jersey Joe Walcott. He fought Billy Conn again and this time beat him early. But his best years were behind him. The knockouts did not come so easily, the reflexes were frayed.

So much had changed in his own life, too. The people closest to him were gone. Marva had filed for divorce during the war. Chappie was dead. The liquor finally ate up his insides. Momma was gone, too.

Joe retired as champion in 1949, but his

debts drove him back to the ring a year later. He lost a unanimous decision to the new champion, Ezzard Charles. He finally ended his career in New York, on October 26, 1951, against a fast-rising contender from Massachusetts named Rocky Marciano, who would go on to be a great heavyweight champion himself, the only one to retire undefeated. But on this night Marciano was just a tough kid fighting his boyhood idol, who was thirty-seven years old, sluggish and weary.

The end came hard and ugly in the eighth. Marciano battered him through the ropes. Joe fell into the arms of his old Detroit friend, Walker Smith. The skinny little kid who had carried Joe's gym bag had kept his promise of someday becoming a fighter, too. His name now was Sugar Ray Robinson, and as the middleweight and welterweight champion he would be considered by many the greatest boxer ever.

Tonight he cradled his old hero's head. "Joe, you'll be all right," he said.

Afterward, Rocky Marciano came to Joe's dressing room in tears. The reporters stood around in silence. Sadness overwhelmed every-

The Brown Bomber meets some Bronx Bombers. The Yankee baseball players are (left to right) Yogi Berra, Allie Reynolds, and Joe DiMaggio. On the far left is Walker Smith, who as a skinny little kid in Detroit carried Joe's gym bag. By now he was better known as Sugar Ray Robinson, world middleweight champ.

one but Joe. He tried to cheer them all up. You
win some, you lose some, he said.

All his life he would evoke emotion from
other people. He retired with a magnificent

record of sixty-eight victories and only three defeats and an unmatched almost twelve years as champion. No matter how sad his later life became, people would always think of him in his finest moments.

To the day he died, on April 12, 1981, he would always be the Joe Louis who beat Carnera and Braddock and Schmeling. His later drinking and gambling problems, his pathetic attempt to pay off his tax debts by wrestling, his failed marriages and his final job, as a greeter in a Las Vegas casino, might have destroyed the memory of anyone else. But when people met Joe, all they could see was the beautiful Brown Bomber who had given them hope.

In Joe Louis's time, America struggled through depression and war and emerged the richest and most powerful nation in the world. He was a symbol of that struggle and of that triumph. He made Jackie Robinson's victories possible, and Muhammad Ali's, too. And when he was champion, it seemed as though he had all the power in the world.

In 1970, when Louis was fifty-five, the sports-

Joe thought Muhammad Ali was a no-talent loudmouth when they first met, and he turned down Ali's invitation to train him. But by 1966, when Ali held the heavyweight title, Ali was on his way to his own place in boxing and world history.

writer Ira Berkow talked to him about that
struggle.

"I think I just come along at a time when
white people began to know that colored people
wouldn't be terrorized no more," he said. "And
the way I carried myself during that comin' up
made some whites begin to look at colored people different."

Louis told Berkow that Jackie Robinson was
his hero for having "the guts" to speak his mind
about racism. Another outspoken hero of Louis's
was Paul Robeson, the great college athlete,
scholar and opera singer. Joe said, "Robeson did
more for the Negroes than anyone else, even
though someone like King did a lot."

It was the Reverend Martin Luther King Jr.
who wrote about a young black man who was
put to death in a Mississippi gas chamber during the time Louis was champion. As the deadly
fumes engulfed him, the young man cried out
for help, not from the Governor or the President
or even God. He cried, "Save me, Joe Louis,
save me, Joe Louis. . . ."

For Dr. King, the story showed the power of

the young boxing champion in a time when hope was hard to find. Joe Louis didn't save that young man, but in his own way, he had given new life and hope to millions.

At Joe's funeral, the Reverend Jesse Jackson said, "God sent Joe Louis from the Black race to represent the human race."

For Further Reading

Astor, Gerald. . . . *And a Credit to His Race.* New York: Saturday Review Press, 1974.

Barrow, Joe Louis, Jr., and Barbara Munder. *Joe Louis: Fifty Years an American Hero.* New York: McGraw Hill, 1988.

Levine, Peter. *American Sport: A Documentary History.* Englewood Cliffs, NJ: Prentice-Hall, Inc., 1989.

Louis, Joe, with Edna and Art Rust, Jr. *Joe Louis: My Life.* New York: Harcourt Brace, 1978.

Mead, Chris. *Champion: Joe Louis: Black Hero in White America.* New York: Scribner's, 1985.

INDEX

Page numbers of photographs appear in *italics*.